MW01537052

This book belongs to

_____

To understand what the outside of an aquarium looks like, it's better not to be a fish. -Andre Malraux

Every day
I am more
peaceful and
happy
than the
day before.

No good fish goes anywhere without a porpoise.

-Lewis Carroll

A fish tank is just interactive television for cats.
- Oliver Gaspirtz

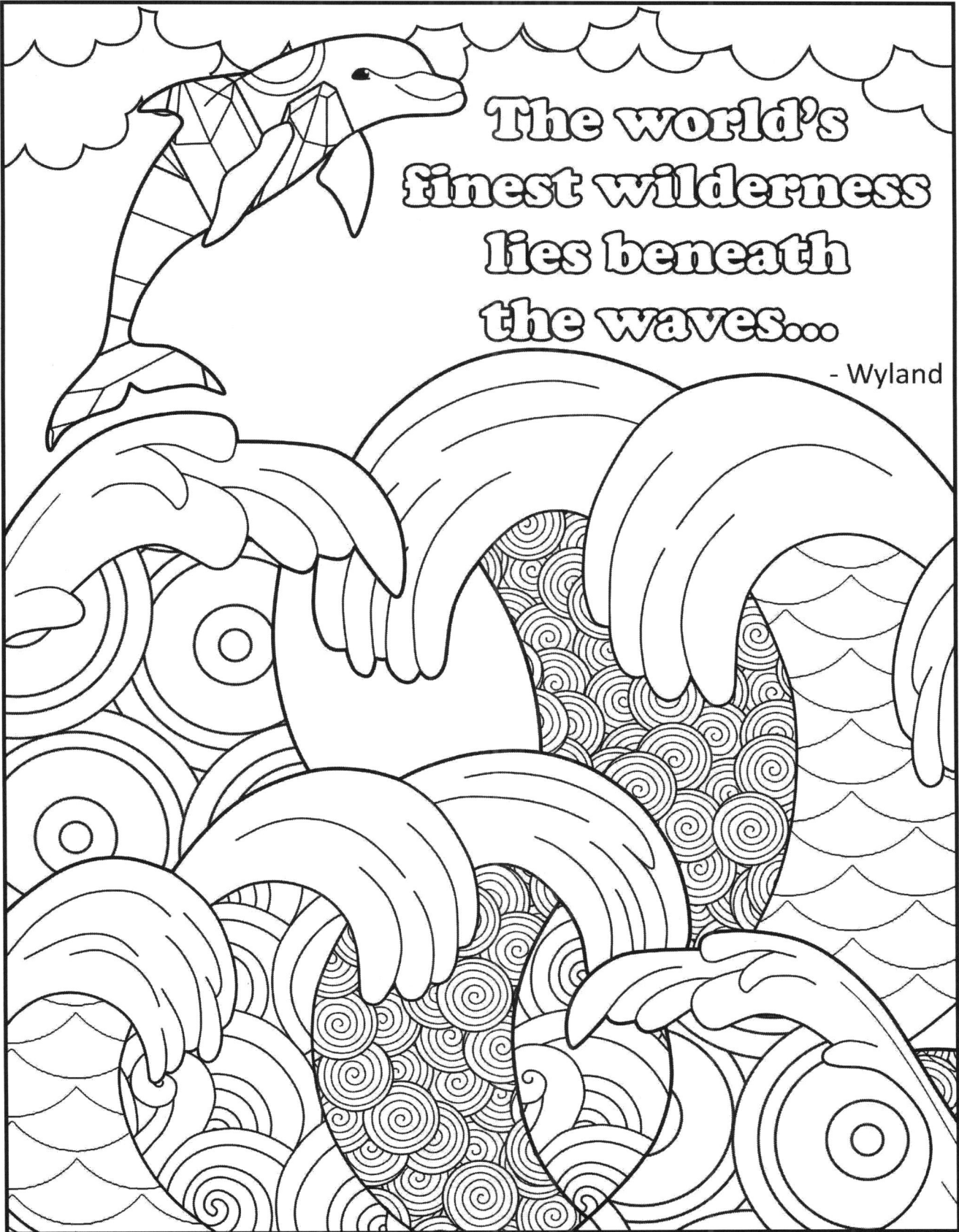

The world's
finest wilderness
lies beneath
the waves...

- Wyland

I always do my best because it helps me grow.

THE BEST WAY TO OBSERVE A FISH IS TO BECOME A FISH.

- Jacques Yves Cousteau, Oceanographer

Made in the USA
Las Vegas, NV
17 February 2022

44109412R00035